LOVER / PRIORY

Adrienne Wilkinson is a poet and a massage therapist. She studied a masters in Poetry at the University of East Anglia. Her first book, *repeating mouths*, was published by Broken Sleep Books in 2021. She lives in Norwich.

Also by Adrienne Wilkinson

repeating mouths (Broken Sleep Books, 2021)

CONTENTS

FLIRTING WITH YOU	7
THE RIDGES ON MY FINGERS FUSCHIA & PEACH	8
RIVER FLOWING UP TO THE HEART, I WANT TO PUT MY HAND IN IT	9
FLOWERS	10
ALONG THE WAY IS A POND	11
BAD WINGS	12
LIGHT LIKE A RIPENING APPLE	15
THERE IS A MOMENT DANCING THRU EVERYTHING & IS IT GOD?	16
READING THE MARKERS OF AUTISM IN GIRLS, I BECOME ♥	17
LOVER / PRIORY	18

ACKNOWLEDGEMENTS	46

© 2025, Adrienne Wilkinson All rights reserved; no part of this book may be reproduced by any means without the publisher's permission.

ISBN:978-1-917617-32-1

The author has asserted their right to be identified as the author of this Work in accordance with the Copyright, Designs and Patents Act 1988

Cover designed by Aaron Kent

Cover image © jozefklopacka/ Adobe Stock

Edited and Typeset by Aaron Kent

Broken Sleep Books Ltd
PO BOX 102
Llandysul
SA44 9BG

lover / priory

Adrienne Wilkinson

Broken Sleep Books

FLIRTING WITH YOU

one of those days where i am kind of
quietly waiting for someone to hit on me
with a body that sometimes steps forward
hoping someone looks over my shoulder
and doesn't ask too many questions
i don't have a name, lets talk
about other things. what is
your favourite fruit?
mine is a cherry

THE RIDGES ON MY FINGERS FUSCHIA & PEACH

i go to the woods

to look for mushrooms

i find mushrooms

i know i shouldn't touch mushrooms

but i touch the mushrooms

in fact i get close with a mushroom

running my finger over the gills

which feel so familiar, gills

like ruched fabric, gills

like a squeezed lemon

rubbery on top

i am surprised it is actually pink underneath

and there, when yesterday it wasn't

RIVER FLOWING UP TO THE HEART, I WANT TO PUT MY HAND IN IT

when you touch me i feel myself as a child or that the creakiness
of my hip has something to do with strength when you touch

your hand on my heart not metaphorically i feel
the power of my rage which expands beyond my edges i feel subtle

emanation the way one life can breathe over
another how another's breathing reverberates how

the people you spend time with share
bacteria through breath & maybe i am sharing breath

with someone impressive or with the capacity to make
big changes & how long would it take someone being

in a trees presence for it to notice their touch i wonder
if i touch one part of a tree for 20 minutes will it sense

me & be able to tell me yes i have pain there yes
that makes me think of when i was a sapling yes

where i was cut into that is the place where i think
i hold my fear & although my heart beat is paced

at a much slower rate than yours as i draw water
from the ground can you feel the pulse relatively racing

FLOWERS

opening reminding me of ovulation yes i want to fuck the spring to be more like spring to become spring until dewy snowdrops unfurl from my stomach daffodils elbow themselves out of my ribcage honeysuckle from my neck yes i want to taste that life stirring within me & wake up stronger feeling the sun's warmth radiate out of me lavendula pooling inside me & my body is turning to dusk later & later so my skin is inky & goosebumped & in the morning birdsong limbers my joints & chest & stirrings underground bring the smell of vetiver from my pores something is building / spring is coming

ALONG THE WAY IS A POND

       acidic water makes an abundance of hagstones

       the stones aren't smoothed with time but rather holed

       like something forceful has happened

       i find 7   in under 10 minutes

       & put all 7 in my pocket running

       my fingers over them as i walk

              each step imagining holes

              spores & bad surprises

BAD WINGS

caterpillar larvae

green against green

leaf and looking kind of limp

and squishy when i feel

    looked on

    almost like there are no

        eyes at all

        like a wriggling spring

            of fat or chewy

            gum not something that

            looks back

    moving very slowly

    taking so much

    effort to get there

        it's a joke

        to be such

        a tiny thing

    which is how i felt

    for most parts of my life

although the softness

came later not until

    i had undergone some

kind of transformation

under striplights

with dogs basically

                wondering

                    who here is secretly

                    secure feeling guilty

                    for the £30 a week

                    child benefit

                passed on from home

as if that was some

kind of

inheritance

☽

    small flower
    pond
        holding hand
    her heart is like a frog in my palm
    i don't know if its skin is burning i don't
    know if we are the same
    i am coming home to her sometimes
        froghearted
            with a swelling need

O

when it is wet
the soil shouts
    iloveyouiloveyou
    fall down over my whole body
    until your body is soil
  at work we talk about growing daisies
  & everyone has mother on their lips

☾

    looking into the deep well
    watching tides turn
    until the centre of earth looks back at you
    knowing what happened in your whole life

LIGHT LIKE A RIPENING APPLE

i am nested in that core

brushing moss from the chairs

smell of ground

       lightening looking

            feeling not very

                    present eye hanging

                              off flower leaf bird

            thinking five senses

            thinking five things

            trying to imagine there

isn't day ahead

            day behind

                    the cold is here

                          and so is light

            i am here now

            i am

here now

THERE IS A MOMENT DANCING THRU EVERYTHING & IS IT GOD?

& there is something that happens when i am walking where it feels like i am staying completely still & the wind is blowing thru me & maybe it is pink sunset & i am no longer ashamed to be obsessed with love

& love is happening on every scale me & you at home with cats dividing up our share of the housework in some kind of way putting the bins out & planting seeds in the garden thinking what if we never have children & the life in the soil is both tender and violent

& when my grandma was ill on my mother's birthday i was thinking about russian dolls & you had discovered that the fallen nest I bought you after your operation held your inner child & you were ready to love her

& there are times when i cry maybe every day or twice a day or times when i dont cry for months & those experiences are happening to the same person & i feel the same in them i feel like i am watching myself & i suppose that is god

& the blush of it is so beautiful i love to see you grumpy & your face is furrowed & i am laughing at you because i love you & when you won't smile at me i become kind of anxious on the outside & kind of anxious on the inside but further inside is a flower garden humming

READING THE MARKERS OF AUTISM IN GIRLS, I BECOME ⱱ

a nun picking roses ⱱ her hands are many small stigmata ⱱ that is the feeling of outside on her skin ⱱ wrapping her head in fabric makes her feel closer to god ⱱ in this version of things god is becoming overwhelmed by her own experience of herself ⱱ her manifestations ⱱ when sunset is pooling down glistening ⱱ rose struck ⱱ the sky is the colour of her old school uniform ⱱ she understands suddenly why it was always so hard ⱱ noisy ⱱ the safety of the stone nunnery of silence ⱱ of not being god getting overwhelmed by the noises of the bus ⱱ the beautiful babies screaming being a tiny drop of water bending ⱱ reflecting endlessly ⱱ maybe she has found the reason why she was able to create something so huge so overwhelming something moving in so many directions of red perfect symmetry then suddenly blood

LOVER / PRIORY

priory

o disciples! circling

glasses like singing angels

tender doubles pouring wine

tracing earth with their feet, eating flesh

open like a squat   what wounds!

i feel like an animal   worse

an animal i dont know, drunken

were they punishing   us /

i feel like unpaid for space   so

many ruined objects! even the rooms

are empty   disciples! like insects

each footstep is monk on their knees

priory,,   your body is what

they are prizing,   palms

weaving desire, close fingers

pocked with prayer

& drops of deep red in the cracks

& wanting,,

lover

i feel closer

to you, touching your feet

hard skin like comfort

thumb to arch walking the priory

of course i find you, that is my

orientation, in terms of attachment

the monks are attached to god

the priory is attached to the ground

                                            pacing our desires by the stone

                                            each footstep, we are here

                                            surrounded by brambles

                                            drinking wine & touching

                                            things gently

priory

is there a hole in that stone?
is that a hagstone?

o stone giver, would you have been hostile to our embraces?
would your disciples have laid their fingers to our endlessly
opening mouths?

                    committed as in devoted to you as in locked
                    up for my own good by enduring powers
                    giving my love to you i am devoted to you
                    priory   walking around this same
                    patch of grass again & again thinking what do
                    dandelions do for soil measuring the
                    dimensions of a field with my feet feeling the
                    desire of my history as in each step is a
                    repetition / as in giving myself to something
                    someone i dont even know   what

priory

approaching you i felt the haul
of stone in my chest   like
the whole world was a ruin,

even the houses were ruins
i walked past three churches & a nursery
i felt like people were looking at me

there was a smell of roses & well
kept shrubbery   all the gates were closed
reconstructed mouth

swallow   the monks here were
secluded, you kept their secrets, the walls
are tall so i cant hop over them,,

small crevice in the wall

small wound

like god has a melon baller

to make beds for a pigeon

like a child in the safety

of the smallest space they can find

who is comfortable in these borders?

who has adapted well

womb stone

the texture is huge & curvaceous

so it feels good around me

so it feels good in my hand

priory

say i see you, imagine you are inside me

with my crumbling walls, yes my body

is the ruinplace of the ritual

repeat your steps, create

those desire lines & imagine the spectres

imagine a building

imagine a persons body, pave me

put yourself in me & build me

with your bricks   lets swap

positions, in what ways

are you worshipped?

in what ways are you better

at the borders?

lengthening grass a hundred small lives in the feet of ants lifting such heavenly things above their small heads so when you look down it seems the earth itself is twitching ladybirds can actually fly but often they chose to walk eating the tender green aphids & creating mythologies of ruins a dog paw crushes a piece of grass dog pisses on the wall & a tug of light bounces off the stream off the glistening rock the beautiful wall the grass grows so someone must be mowing but they cant quite get close enough to the wall to get right into that fruitful space squashed black juice bottle top childs shoe crisp packet empty vodka bottle even a stone which has fallen down looks up at the womb the building the ruin which is now there as an object of interest as an empty cup

so you are coming to know me

so there is nothing that cannot change

so you can feel the swarm of your skin

priory

those small stairs are telling me secrets

which monk sat hunched like a screwed up fist

stone walls curling around saying *o i see you*

saying *o i wont burn long enough*

under i was a child hunching in that upward cupboard counting
prayers on my fingers letting water run over waiting to tonguehush
the keen dusk of a blackberry actually edging counting numbers
on my body thinking thirteen fourteen fifteen under i was a child
clutching small surprises badly

which stair is pacing you out
?

                                                what   a

                                                strang

                                                e child!

lover

        your small hands are fruitfully reflective
           as i move mine up down over under
        as mine find their way through the rubble
      this ungodly mess! its good to see you in it
              your body is the shape of a psalm
              your body is the shape of a satsuma
              your body is the shape of a communion
                      wafer

i dont even care anymore / i just want to do that thing again

lover

its not really the place but

i am not ashamed to tell you what i am thinking

the only prayer that makes sense is you & your mischief / we are always thanking god its not so serious in the moments that we realise parts of our lives actually have been harder stonier more pocked more ruin / i dont feel ashamed to tell you

about times so fitting for a scorpio or to know the selfish awful things embarrassing desperate things i have done / making bodies from the dust of our bedclothes making houses like hermit crabs robed by salt robed by stone

priory

the ruined staircase spirals inward
in shell like fractals
the hermit i imagine there
is looking for something to
trouble his stillness

he looks like a spiral himself
beneath his burning
oil lamp   such impressive
stillness!   likehis
body is made itself
of calcium carbonate

the holes in the walls like
pocks, teeth
and bone   frail
his thinness is astounding
reminding   thinness

reserved for the past
for death, shocking
even coldest hardest

,,

the hermit does not look

to one side or the other

he is the edge of the border

watching

priory

inside the hermit says *o My Lord God, I have no idea where I am going. I do not see the road ahead of me, nor do i really know myself. And the fact that I think that I am following your will, does not mean that I am actually doing so. But I believe that the desire to please you, does in fact please you. And I hope that I will never do anything apart from that desire. And I know that if i do this, you will lead me by the right road, though I may know nothing about it. Therefore I will trust you always, though i seem to be lost and in the shadow of death. I will not fear for you are ever with me, and you will never leave me to face my struggles alone.*

what animal AM i?

lover

i have no idea where i am going

                        the basket of your interwoven fingers
                              the desire to please you
                                      hermit crab
                                        oil lamp
                        this astounding concealment
                                         glasses
                                like singing angels
                                opening mouth,,   o
                                      hagstone
                         empty rooms, empty rooms

you
resisting, enticing movement
                    like a border

lover

        when i look at your skin right now it is simply a swarm

                we are a stones throw from the sea

you throw your cloaked head back in
laughter when i put my hands in that holy
water home soaked   come further
let us hop on over

                      i look along,, all i see is borders

lover

would you put your finger to the stone?

would you trace along its edges?

would you pledge yourself to its ornate corners?

when i pause on those borders i see swarms

the ants astounding strength imagine the whole priory was built by ants the smallest thing could build anything holding up crumbling walls bodies tense against the pressure even the father was built by the strength of tiny creatures swarming holding up something ten times one hundred times their size yes i believe my desire to please you does in fact please you following one step after following that desire following the glances & shards in the grass i am too small for them to hurt me legs scratching from every part of my body these long lines these desires this astounding strength & stony hardness

                    how still can one

                    child be?   where

                    are the children

                    here?

                            they turned

                  to stones

                          see,, they are good for skipping

priory

what i wanted from you was a home

a way to understand masculine as
sanctuary

to know the quiet dignity of men in
service

but i imagine them here in the latrine
shitting side by side

& facing their own darkness, what they call
need for god

squat open, drop to god, their skinny
bodies itchy

                                          your small nooks
                                          offer another opening

—

        you are just as lost
        as i am!   hermit!
        your lantern is no guide
        to me i see nothing by it!
        i see ants & edges i see
        nothing but desire

the light grows the grass inside the rooms

                the rooms themselves are

                empty

lover

standing in front of an empty doorway

you are on the other side, a mirror

o doorway! with grass inside, my
feet directly on the ground this
floor is alive! is the same
as outside you inside is the
same as outside if i step
through that passing place what
changes why do i believe this
what do i believe about
you what happens when i
love you? just that on the
inside you seem to be me o
doorway o lover you are so
incredibly so astonishingly
still as i love you love that
stone of you tell me were you
a child? the same on the
inside i skip you to sea o this
doorway what wonders pass
through it! you stand on one
side i stand on the other our
hands meet in the passing
place on the border in that
rivulet of light & as we look past our hands we see the swarm of
our skin we see that all things are breathing we see the grey stone
skipping the pale blue surface saying up   up   up

lover

following
    my footsteps
        i begin to get the feeling
            i dont know how many times
                i will circle this stone

i get the feeling
    you are a border
        i can never cross
           wind in the grass like serpents
                grass full of tucked away things

rubbing my thumb
    over a small hag stone
        fallen debris
           holy stone
                my thumb reflecting
                    the moves of my feet

rying to find a comfort
    in this ruin
        trying to know
            the stillness of stone
                the value of worship

the body of ritual

    the spit & blood of it

        my thumb goes inside the stone

            is bedded in the empty

                space

i do not know where i am going

        each footstep is a life

            heartbeat

                empty   womb

priory

in the middle of the archway i see

the shame of a masturbating child i

have taken long strides to get here

now she is there just to be looked at

light from her lantern illuminates her

solar plexus   i dont really know

her spectring / but i know her exactly

in her wounds   wine glasses singing

all around   with a look like somebody

has whispered in her ear

she shouts *im scared* she shouts *leave me*

alone   a voice replies *YOU are shouting,*

so who is the scary one?

on my thumb the hagstone is soft,

i will never be anything apart from that

she eats blackberries hushed
her lips become purple & pink
with animal rapidity

sugar coats her fingers & belly
i suppose the ants are coming she
doesnt really care / i see nothing
but desire   she just wants to skip
on the pale surface

she just wants to walk
like a heartbeat   in circles
what a strange child!   she just
wants to walk   like a heartbeat
in circles

lover

in the sea smoothed pebbles & stones are rolling like heartbeats with the waves in the arms of that ever swelling swallowing that pale blue taker endlessly reflecting those punctures those ravines of light wine glasses angels singing i remember the first time you swam i could see the child in your eyes that holy bowler blew you away your swaying edges sea soaked that swarm was soothed you murmured like a baby like grass growing in a glance murmuring like ribbons of wind on the surface

>
> a lantern in one hand the hermit
> is still calling
>
> performing vigils, lauds, prime, terce, sext, none, vespers, compline
>
> endless like angels
> voice like calcium carbonate

in your eyes i see the stone of you
in your eyes i see those empty rooms

lover

to be in love is so unserious, empty
rooms are filled, until we leave

i am proud of all those ghosts, i liked
when you told me how your

sad childhood made you feel
mine made me feel different

to that, when i hold your hand
usually it falls away after while

when i hold my pain, usually
it falls away like a stone, sinking

        like a small animal, digging
        like the drop could save me

        like beneath those cold foundations
        there is a dark warm burrow

        the shape of my body, doubled

priory

        i leave you, counting

    prayers on my fingers, plucking

    blackberries from the bramble

        barbed & drunken

          i walk,   open

           as a heart, washed

              as a stone

ACKNOWLEDGEMENTS

Thank you Aaron Kent and the team at Broken Sleep Books.

Tiffany Atkinson, Sophie Robinson and Holly Corfield Carr, thank you for your time and guidance.

Thank you Lauren Sheerman for reading my poems and inspiring me with yours.

To my friends, family and loved ones, thank you for the endless support

LAY OUT YOUR UNREST

www.ingramcontent.com/pod-product-compliance
Lightning Source LLC
Chambersburg PA
CBHW030814090426
42737CB00010B/1275